Coping with Loss

An Introduction to Loss and Loss Counselling

by

Roy V Lascelles

Second Edition

ISBN 0 948680 21 0

Dedication:

To Brian Goodall, for his patience and tolerance.

Give sorrow words. The grief that does not speak
Whispers the o'erfraught heart and bids it break.

Macbeth, Act 4 Scene 3
William Shakespeare

Contents Guide

The Author

Roy Lascelles began his social work career in 1975 and studied for the CQSW at Croydon College of Design and Technology. After several years as a generic area-based social worker, he worked in a general hospital which included a geriatric rehabilitation unit, a day hospital and maternity unit. After a number of years as a Senior Social Worker with a local authority, Roy has been working part-time in social work and part-time "self-or unemployed", as he describes it himself.

Acknowledgements

My grateful thanks go to Andrew Berryman for his encouragement to me in my work; to Elizabeth (Betty) James and Mavis Hill for accepting the daunting task of typing the manuscript and correcting my spelling; and finally to all my past clients who have contributed, unwittingly, to the production of this work.

Roy V Lascelles *December 1990*

Preface

Dying and death are not everyday topics of conversation; they are mostly regarded as morbid and best ignored and hence they are unfamiliar issues for many people. Paradoxically death is a fact of life, but it still elicits embarrassment and defensive attitudes, perhaps because death is often associated with pain, fear, ugliness and hopelessness. We may not know how best to console a person who is bereaved and we may be unable to understand or cope with our own reactions to other people's disturbing and unpredictable behaviour. There are very few set guidelines on how to behave in such a situation.

My interest in loss counselling was stimulated while working as a hospital social worker when I discovered how often unresolved grief seemed to be the cause behind the presenting symptoms of those people referred to me by the medical staff for help.

The interest of other workers in my profession became clear when, in 1984, I was asked to present a two-day course of in-service training on the subject of loss counselling.

Attention should be given to the role of social workers as counsellors, for they are well placed to make an effective contribution to this area of work through their training and knowledge of personal development and functioning. Some people would say that because social workers have the relevant knowledge and practice skills they should have a professional obligation to provide a service for people suffering from loss reaction. I would not have written this book if I did not agree with that. Social workers are well equipped to provide a service in this area of need, and they meet loss in their clients' lives in many situations, not only when bereaved. Think about receiving or taking children into care, transferring elderly clients from their own homes to residential accommodation, stillbirths and termination of pregnancy, amputees, divorce and separation, loss of job and redundancy - the list is endless.

The contents of this book are a compilation of theories and practice I have encountered during the period of my work with the bereaved, from courses I have attended, extensive reading on the subject and my own clients' experiences.

My hope is that this book will provide a repertoire of skills and techniques to be used when appropriate, rather than a fixed plan of action, for helping those who have suffered a significant loss.

Roy V. Lascelles
Mitcham, Surrey

December, 1990

Introduction

The model and method of application presented in this book may be used in bereavement work; however the counselling skills discussed may also be used in helping people who have suffered any major loss. The loss may be of an object, a limb, an organ, a person or a relationship, and clearly some losses will represent a bigger threat to our wellbeing than others. Sometimes there will be not just one loss but a whole series of deprivations to which a person has to adjust.

There are infinite human responses to a major loss situation and it is impossible to deal with them all in one small book. In the following chapters, while I shall be dealing with bereavement in particular, it is important to remember that the principles explained are easily adapted to other crisis situations or loss and change in general. In addition, the practical techniques which will be discussed may be useful in any interviewing situation.

In the past, extended families and the neighbourhood, together with the church, provided a close community which helped people cope with a loss. Because many people no longer belong to a religious organisation and easier mobility has moved family members long distances away from each other, a sense of strong community may no longer exist; so people now turn to the social care system for the support which previously came from other sources.

Death may no longer be the common family experience it was in previous centuries and many rituals are no longer observed. Times have changed since the days when a dead person was laid out in the parlour, when all who wanted to could come and say goodbye. Very few people now wear black armbands to show they have suffered a loss. People think twice about letting very young children attend a funeral and they say things like "Daddy's gone to sleep" or "Granny's passed over"; but Daddy has not gone to sleep and Granny has not passed over; they have died and that means they are not coming back.

Facing reality is very important if someone is to work through their grief. To deny the truth leads to complications. If the truth is accepted, everyone knows where they stand and adapting to the changed circumstances can begin.

Death has become a 'taboo' subject in society with the result that many normal reactions to bereavement, such as 'seeing' or talking with the dead person, are thought of as signs of madness which incurs the raising of unnecessary anxiety. Bereavement is a normal part of living involving, albeit more intensely, our normal reactions and feelings.

Change of status takes place many times during the course of our lives, and crisis events are characteristic of the normal growth and development of an individual. We pass through successive stages, such as learning to walk and talk, going to school, moving through puberty, getting our first job, courtship, marriage, having children, illness, death of relatives, retirement, old age and finally our own death. In addition to such normal crises, people may also experience events like domestic tragedy, redundancy, injury leading to permanent disability, or being rejected in love.

These events can and may lead to the further growth of individuals if they are able to work through the emotional disturbance and develop their character and personality.

We have all had some experience of loss and change in our lives, and it is these experiences that we have worked through and come through which we can draw on to be empathetic and aware of others' feelings when they too have suffered a loss.

What I hope to do in the following chapters is to set some guidelines which will help in practice and stimulate some thinking about how counsellors may become more able to judge if what they are doing is appropriate. No two losses manifest in the same way and similar losses may bring different reactions from different people; therefore help which is beneficial for one person may not be for another.

Loss counselling is important because, in this day and age, it is sometimes difficult to know how to react to others when we or they are very unhappy.

People seek help or are referred for help when they feel they cannot cope alone with their grief or that their grief will never end. They may have no insight into their future and need help to return to some sort of equilibrium, albeit different from before the loss occurred. Grief often manifests through various physical or mental conditions, so people may be referred to a counsellor without recognising that there may be a grief reaction underlying their particular debilitating condition.

A lot of what we will be doing when we talk to people who have suffered a loss is putting them in touch with their feelings and helping to make them easier to handle. Therefore we need to be aware of our own strengths and weaknesses. This does not mean that we need to go into analysis, but if we have just lost or separated from our husband or wife it could well be difficult to be objective about someone else's grief if we are still tied up with our own.

If we have difficulty handling other people's anxieties and distress, this can impinge on our own anxiety and heighten it. Confrontation with those who have suffered a loss is likely to engender feelings of anxiety, confusion and uncertainty in ourselves.

We really need to be aware of our own emotions and what we are able to handle emotionally. Working with the bereaved can and may unleash strong emotions and reactions. I do not wish to imply that we have to remain cool, calm, collected and aloof at all times, for that would be inhuman, but a good philosophy to remember is that it is all right to cry with the client but it is not all right to lose control.

To help others through their loss we need basic skills and interviewing techniques. Practical methods for making things easier in our work are always useful. We need to look at what we are doing, why we are doing it and how we can make a success of it.

In the following chapters I will present a model for separating a whole person into pieces or dimensions so that, while we are working with them, we can examine how they are coping in each of these dimensions. We will look at what they might be experiencing and going through after a major loss and seeking long-term aims to help them move to a more healthy outlook and way of life. With this model we can isolate the areas or dimensions which need attention if long-term aims are to be achieved.

We shall go on to explore the wide range of situations and events in which people can experience strong loss reactions. Crises visit us all, and often we are left at the end with less than we had. The consequent grief has to be handled appropriately if people are to grow through crises rather than be demolished by them.

We will then look at several practical techniques which will facilitate our communication with the client and also help both ourselves and the client to work on the dimensions which need attention.

Finally we will look at the counselling process and the stages which we, the counsellors, need to pass through with the client during their loss adjustment period.

The first four chapters of this book should form a basis from which loss counselling may be implemented for the benefit of the client and ourselves as counsellors.

To summarise, we shall:-

a) look at the changes taking place in clients during their loss adjustment period and our long-term aims to help them through this period,

b) explore those crises events which can often be the cause of strong loss reactions,

c) practise some of the skills we need in order to communicate with the client and help the client communicate with us, and

d) look at the process of counselling and what, as counsellors, we should be doing.

TABLE 1

SUMMARY OF DIMENSIONS

Dimension	Reactions	Goals
Intellectual	Disbelief Denial	Acceptance of the fact of the loss and its implications. Adapting to changed circumstances. Resolving conflict between past and future purpose and habits.
Psychological	Disbelief/Acceptance Idealisation Guilt/Anger Shock/Confusion Hallucinations	Formation of new identity and self-concept. Realisation of potential for healthier adjustment to future crises and stress
Spiritual	Crisis of faith Suicidal thoughts Regression/Helplessness Displaced Anxiety/Blame	Redefine the meaning of life. Restoration of will and creation of purpose to carry on.
Physical	Stress/Pain Numbness/Fatigue Sleep disturbance Loss of appetite Lack of exercise Stress-reduction addiction	Promotion of physical health and reduction of stress-related illness.
Emotional	Sadness/Crying Guilt/Anger Defensiveness/Repression Thoughts of Madness Yearning for past Emotional withdrawal/ Avoidance Negative Attitude Relief	Release of emotional tension. Restoring emotional equilibrium.
Behavioural	Irrational behaviour Aimlessness/Restlessness Absentmindedness Social withdrawal/Isolation Avoidance of reality	Lower distress. Changing inappropriate behaviour to minimise disrupted lifestyle and reorganising habitual patterns and routines.
Social	Uncertainty/Confused behaviour Isolation/Loneliness Sorrow/Disappointment	Acceptance of new role and reorganising family structure. Resolving family conflicts and status. Establishing independence and new relationships. Putting others at ease, feeling comfortable.
Practical	Helplessness Anxiety/Confusion	Avoiding major life changes. Adapting to practical demands of daily living.

Chapter One

Dimensions of Adjustments

Introduction

In this chapter the term 'mourning' refers to the process which occurs after a loss and the term 'grief' refers to the personal experience of the loss. As mourning is a process, it may be seen in terms of stages or phases; other people writing about grief reactions have listed several stages of grief. It is important to remember when learning the 'stages' that they may not necessarily occur consecutively and that people may not pass through them in natural sequence. There is a tendency for someone who is beginning to counsel to take the stages too literally. I would not disagree at all with the 'stages' principle of mourning but wish to illustrate, in this chapter, that the ***Dimensions of Adjustment Model*** which I present is just as valid for understanding the mourning process and may be of real use to the practitioners of grief work counselling. This model implies that the mourning process can be influenced by intervention from a good counsellor who is able to give the mourning person some sense of control and hope, that there is something they can actively do with their grief rather than passively wait for the 'stages' to pass.

Major loss is a very complex issue and people experience their grief in many different ways which can vary in intensity from person to person. In this chapter, loss counsellors are presented with a grief work model in an easily understandable form. Although it is presented in a simple way, I do not wish to imply that mourning is a simple process. I will portray a picture of what people may experience following a loss and some of the reasons why they do so. The chapter will show the tasks people may need to tackle to help them pass through their grief and how the counsellor may identify the problem areas in the mourning process in order to lead to a restoration of equilibrium.

After a major loss is sustained, there are certain tasks which must be completed to regain equilibrium and for the mourning process to be accomplished. All human growth is influenced by accomplishing various tasks. If the tasks are not completed fully, adapting to a new way of life may be impaired as a person may not move on successfully to other tasks later in life.

Adapting to loss involves the accomplishment of the tasks listed later in the Dimensions. Although the tasks described need not follow in my written order, there is some order suggested by their headings and the explanations given. For example, the first dimension listed is the Intellectual Dimension as people will not be able to cope with the Emotional Dimension of a loss until they have come to terms with the fact that the loss has actually occurred.

It is possible for many people to accomplish unaided some or most or even all of the tasks described, but some people may not be able to complete all tasks alone; therefore incomplete mourning will occur, leading to distorted or abnormal grieving.

Our social sub-cultures provide us with some guidelines and rituals for behaviour. For example, the Italians grieve differently to the Irish. Protestants have their own rituals, as do Catholics. For counsellors to predict how a person may grieve, they need to know something about the social, ethnic and religious background of the mourner.

All dimensions of personality need to be considered in an adjustment period. We need to look for a balanced picture and not just concentrate on bad reactions. Remember, there is no clear progression through grief. By separating the whole person into a series of dimensions, we can examine how they are coping in each area of their life. We may find that some areas of the person's life are working well while others are not. Using the Dimensions of Adjustment model will make it easier to isolate those that need attention in order to lead to a total resolution of grief and to a restoration of functional ability.

The Dimensions

The first three dimensions, Intellectual, Psychological and Spiritual, may be grouped together under a sub-heading, ***Mental,*** but they are explained separately as each dimension has its own slight variants.

Intellectual Dimension

Bereaved persons need to accept the fact of the loss and acknowledge the implications of it before they will be able to move on to reorganising their life. They will need to think through the changes which will result from their loss. They may well feel a threat to their established structure of ideas and thinking. They will need to enter into a process of examining their life, unlearning old habits and learning new ones. Their conservative impulses may resist change, but they will have to attempt to make sense of the loss and fit into a new status and their changed place in the world. A wife now becomes a widow, a mother now becomes childless; part of their ordered world is now missing.

Initially there will be ***disbelief*** about the event. "It's not true", "I don't believe it", are common phrases to be heard immediately after a major loss.

The way to help at this time is to encourage the bereaved to talk about the loss. Such questions as "Where did he die?", "How did it happen?", "Who was at the funeral?" will help the person talk specifically about the circumstances of the death. It may be painful for them to relive the event before they come to a full awareness of what has happened.

What really matters is not only the fact of the loss but also the meaning of the loss. Some people may protect themselves from reality by ***denying*** the meaning of the loss. This allows the loss to be seen as less significant than it actually is. Some people may immediately throw away clothes, photographs and personal belongings which remind them of the deceased. This can minimise the loss and may be accompanied by such comments as "I don't miss her". By disposing of reminders of the deceased, the bereaved protect themselves from the reality of the loss and may go on to believe that the dead person never existed. This may seem extreme but it is often found that some people will conveniently forget important facts about the deceased to ease the emotional pain which accompanies the memory. It is usual for bereaved persons to wish for a reunion with the deceased, thereby hoping that they have not really died. In the normal mourning process, such thoughts pass fairly quickly, allowing the bereaved to move on through the process.

We must allow the bereaved to accept the fact of bereavement, by talking about their loss and by resolving the conflict between past and future purpose and habits in order that they may restructure their world. In this way their thoughts of the loss will be lessened and they will begin to get rid of inappropriate thoughts and habits, such as still talking to the dead person and still laying their place at the table. Although these thoughts are not uncommon or abnormal in recently bereaved people, they should not persist. However, until someone has accepted the fact of the loss, it is difficult for them to think of life without the dead person.

Psychological Dimension

This dimension is concerned with the thoughts, feelings and needs of the person suffering a loss. Once the fact of the loss has been accepted, the bereaved can start to form a new identity and self-concept.

Already, in this second dimension, we can note how the dimensions overlap and cannot be entirely separated for, at this time, even though the bereaved has moved on from ***disbelief*** to some ***acceptance*** of the fact of the loss, there may still be a preoccupation with the image of the dead person and this may be similar to day-dreaming. The bereaved may find this comforting and yet disturbing. They may see someone, when they are out, who reminds them of the dead person and they may need to remind themselves that they really have been bereaved. They may feel a threat to their self-identity and use personality defence mechanisms to protect their integrity.

At this time some people feel much pain. Some will ***deny*** the pain and cut off their true feelings about the dead person. They may do this by ***idealising*** the dead person, remembering only the good things that made them happy and forgetting unpleasant thoughts. To overcome this, a counsellor needs to allow the bereaved to retrieve a balanced picture of the past relationship. Counsellors will often ask a bereaved person to tell them what they miss about the deceased and usually the answers will be of good times and pleasant memories. To obtain a balanced picture and allow the client to see reality, I often ask "Is there anything you don't miss about him/her? This is usually met with a look of surprise and hurt, but eventually the client will remember the dirty washing left lying around and the mud on the carpet, etc., etc., thus regaining a more suitable and appropriate memory of the deceased.

There is a danger that this approach may raise negative thoughts and feelings about the deceased which may incur guilt in the bereaved, so it is important not to leave the client with all negative thoughts but a good balance between the negative and positive images of the deceased.

Anger is commonly expressed after a major loss, and this feeling may confuse the bereaved. They have loved the deceased and are now angry that they have been left. Anger, at this time, comes from a frustration that the bereaved had no control over the situation and could not prevent the death. It is usual for some blame to be laid on others, e.g. the hospital, the doctor, and sometimes even themselves for not doing all they could have done. Here, ***anger*** and ***guilt*** will be combined. Again, a person can be helped by talking over the events and reinforcing that all that was possible was done, so that the anger, guilt and blame are lessened.

Shock will occur most often in the case of a sudden death, but a person who has lost a partner after a long hospitalisation can still experience shock when the death finally occurs. Several people I have known in my work have told me that they knew the patient was going to die but they were never able to prepare themselves enough and still felt shocked and numb when the news finally came.

All these feelings can only add up to *confusion* in the bereaved. They may not be able to order their thoughts and will have difficulty concentrating. They are still in the phase where they will sense the presence of the deceased, hear them and talk to them. *Hallucinations* are not uncommon at this time but will become less intense as time goes on. Prolonged hallucinations may be deemed abnormal, although I have experience of a woman who, some six years after her husband's death, still 'sees' a light over his side of the bed. As she finds this comforting, not disturbing, and her other dimensional states have reached equilibrium, I am not over-concerned about her psychological adjustment. For her, the light will always be there and it reassures her that her husband is safe and still caring for her. Death ends a life but it need not end a relationship.

For someone to move toward a healthy psychological adjustment, we need to help them talk, to form a new identity and become accustomed to it. If this is successful, there will be a realisation of potential for healthier adjustment to future crises or stress.

Spiritual Dimension

When using the word 'spiritual', I do not only mean pertaining to religion and the church, although this is extremely important to bereaved persons if they do have close contact with a religious organisation. I use 'spiritual' to illustrate the general purpose of life and its meaning. A recently bereaved person may well wonder why this has happened to them and may question their purpose to go on alone. They will need to create meaning from their suffering when, perhaps, there will be a crisis of faith: "Why has God done this to me?"

When a significant person has been lost, there is a tendency to regress, to feel helpless and unable to exist without the dead person. The ***anxiety*** displayed needs to be identified to resolve it healthily. Sometimes this anxiety is displaced on to other people, and blame may be laid on the hospital, the doctor or even God. Such people need help to realise that their confusion is a normal reaction to grief.

Suicidal thoughts may not be uncommon; this possibility must be recognised. The counsellor needs to look for signs of change of habits and lifestyle; are there sleeping tablets, tranquillisers or alcohol when there were none before? We should not presume that all bereaved people will feel suicidal or act out the thought, but it is wise to be aware of the possibility and test it out in some way. A simple question like "How do you see the future?" may allow a client to confide their true feelings of hopelessness, or not, as the case may be.

At this time we need to encourage clients to restore their will to live without the dead person and they may need help to redefine the meaning of their life and create a purpose for them to go on.

Physical Dimension

We cannot be sure how someone will respond to stress; therefore we should be constantly aware that there is a danger from accumulated stress as it lowers immune defences.

Aches and pains caused by emotional stress are common. Physical stress is real and not all in the mind. Changes take place in the body due to stress and the symptoms are real. They are physical sensations associated with grief reaction and need to be worked through, as do all the other reactions referred to in the Dimensions of Adjustment.

We have already mentioned pain and confusion in previous Dimensions, and *fatigue* may be experienced as apathy, listlessness or other mood disturbances. Bereaved people often report feeling ***numb,*** which may be due to the shock experienced immediately after a loss. Numbness may also be a defence used to protect the bereaved from all the bad feelings which can be aroused at this time.

General feelings of tightness in the chest, hollowness in the stomach, dry mouth and sore throat, lack of energy and weakness may all be experienced together or separately. Many of these physical feelings will be due to the psychological condition of the bereaved but may also be contributed to by their now disorganised lifestyle.

It is not at all unusual for people in the early stages of mourning to experience ***sleep disturbance*** or ***lack of sleep.*** They may have difficulty getting to sleep and/or wake up early. Usually sleep patterns will correct themselves in time, but some medication may be needed in the short-term.

A client of mine whose husband died spent the first three years after his death waking at 2.30am, the time of his death, and could not get back to sleep. After some counselling she still woke at 2.30am each morning but, because her bad feelings about that time were readjusted and more comfortable to handle, she was able to return to sleep and awake later feeling refreshed.

Loss of appetite is another common physical manifestation of grief. Some people may overeat, but it is more common for people to lose their appetite. Many people 'pick' at food and for some time may only eat snacks. When they are used to cooking for two, they may have difficulty readjusting to shopping and cooking for one; practical help may be needed to make this easier.

Lack of exercise may well lead to reduced appetite and feelings of debility. A bereaved person may have difficulty leaving the home for fear of meeting friends or neighbours who might discuss the deceased, thus causing emotional upset. Some bereaved people stay in bed for most of the day for they can see no purpose in getting up.

Stress reduction addiction through smoking, drinking or drug-taking to excess may occur, and this can exacerbate the physical condition.

It is thus easy to see that poor health is inevitable for those who fail to establish some sort of routine for adequate nourishment, exercise and rest. The promotion of physical health during this time is vital to give the bereaved the strength to use their mental capacities and carry on with the practicalities of their daily life.

Emotional Dimension

Depression and grief both display symptoms such as sleep disturbance, loss of appetite and intense ***sadness***, but in grief reaction there is not the loss of self-esteem usually found in clinical depression. Bereaved people do not usually regard themselves any less because of the loss. The ***guilt*** experienced may well be associated with a specific aspect of the loss rather than a general sense of total self-blame. In grief, a morbid preoccupation with worthlessness is uncommon.

After a significant loss people may feel they are going ***mad;*** hearing voices and seeing images of the dead person (Psychological Dimension) can be very disturbing and are not normally part of their lives. It is essential for the counsellor to have a clear understanding that this is part of normal grief behaviour and give reassurance about the normality of these new and frightening experiences.

There are times when ***sadness*** and ***crying*** need to be encouraged by the counsellor. Men find it particularly difficult to show their emotions, especially in front of women. After a loss they may find it hard to cry and express their true feelings, and yet it is very important that they are helped to do so. People working with men who are bereaved must be particularly sensitive to this need. Often people refuse to cry in front of friends for fear of straining the friendship and perhaps losing those friends. This would be an added loss which would be unbearable. Crying may also be stifled to avoid criticism from others. People who are not aware of how badly a bereaved person feels may be insensitive and make remarks like "Pull yourself together", "It's been three months now, you should be over it", or "Don't be so self-pitying". Comments like these will not help at all and do not offer the support needed; this can lead to more defences being erected, thus suppressing painful feelings. As we have seen in the Physical Dimension, stress causes imbalance in the body and tears can be seen as a physical safety valve as well as an emotional one.

Crying alone may be useful to the bereaved, but it is better if they can cry with someone they trust and receive some support. Counsellors should help by identifying, with the client, the meaning of the tears and thereby clarifying that it is a natural reaction to a sad situation.

Yearning for the deceased is a normal response often encountered. Even when the loss is fully acknowledged (Intellectual Dimension) the bereaved may still wish for a reunion and need to be close to the dead person in some way. The reason for this may be that the bereaved has a fear of losing the memory of the deceased. I have known people deliberately carry a photograph of the deceased "in case I forget what he looked like". When this yearning starts to fade, it is a good sign that the bereaved is making progress and moving on through the mourning process.

If the deceased suffered a long and painful illness, the bereaved may have an initial sense of ***relief***. Usually this feeling is short-lived as other emotions replace it, but it may also arouse some ***guilt*** at the thought of being pleased that a loved one has died.

We have seen that we can expect people to be ***angry,*** for it is a healthy sign to be annoyed if our security is threatened (e.g. reaction to redundancy or housing development), so we should expect this much more if someone has lost the security of someone they have loved.

One of the most difficult tasks for a bereaved person may be to accomplish an ***emotional withdrawal*** from the deceased so that emotions may be transferred to another relationship. They may feel that they are doing a disservice to the deceased if they withdraw the emotional attachment; they may even feel they are violating their memory. They may be wary of starting another relationship for fear of suffering another loss. Some people feel that they married for life and will not be able to love somebody else, so cannot even consider other relationships. They may come into conflict with their children and close relatives if they do choose to start another relationship too soon after a bereavement. However, holding steadfastly on to the past relationship may hinder the grieving process, and the bereaved may have difficulty moving on from the point in their lives when the loss occurred. If they can be helped to withdraw emotionally from the dead person, it will be easier for them to realise that there are other people to be loved and that this does not mean that they love the deceased any less.

We may find that, by trying to help someone who has recently suffered a major loss, they appear to get worse before they get better. Immediately after their loss they may appear controlled and subdued (remember the ***denial, disbelief*** and ***numbness*** from the previous Dimensions which may cause this appearance). Defences lead to blocking growth, so they need to be lowered to help the grieving process. Sometimes a more appropriate defence is needed so that the client still retains some sense of control. Eventually they should start to let go of their defences and it may appear that they are getting worse as their real emotions come to the surface. They will be aware of many frightening and disruptive emotions, but this will lead to growth and eventually a restoration of a more healthy outlook.

Negative and painful responses need to be acknowledged and accepted; we should not detract from these and try to input positives. We should allow the client to lose control in a safe environment, but this can only be done after a good relationship is developed and should only be done if we, the counsellors, are able to accept a flood of emotion. To help the bereaved release disruptive emotions, we need to assure them of trust and safety to make them more comfortable.

Working through disturbing emotions instead of ***denying, avoiding*** and ***repressing*** them will release emotional tension and help restore equilibrium.

Behavioural Dimension

Irrational behaviour is common during the mourning period. To call it irrational might imply that it is abnormal, but it is not. Strange behaviour is experienced by many bereaved people and it usually tends to diminish in frequency and intensity as they come to terms with the change in their life. Some people may actually gain comfort from the experience of seeing and hearing a dead person, but it should be remembered that others will be upset by this phenomenon.

Habitual patterns may not be abandoned immediately after a loss. These actions will still hold meaning until the reality of the loss is grasped and accepted, but the bereaved will need to examine their behaviour and unlearn old habits and learn new and more appropriate ones. Lifestyle will now be disorganised and patterns of habitual behaviour may be broken. The bereaved may be ***aimless*** and ***restless*** and everyday activities become an effort. At this time, people may work against themselves and appear helpless by not developing the new skills they will need, or seclude themselves from the world and not face up to their everyday living needs. Referring back to the Physical Dimension, we may note disruption of sleeping, eating and exercise patterns.

Anxiety, at this time, can vary from person to person and may manifest itself as anything from a sense of insecurity to a strong panic. The anxiety may be because the bereaved feel they will not be able to take care of themselves or take on the tasks performed by the deceased, who perhaps dealt with financial matters, did the cooking, managed the children when they misbehaved, etc. There are many tasks that are shared in a relationship and many that are divided. Suddenly to have to take on someone else's responsibilities as well as your own may well appear too demanding at a time when emotionally, physically and psychologically you are at a low ebb.

In elderly people, anxiety may be more acute as they may now become aware of their own mortality after the death of a spouse.

Absent-minded behaviour is not at all uncommon for, while people are feeling aimless and anxious, concentration will be difficult. They may find themselves repeating tasks continually, having forgotten they have already done something or forgetting an important task until it is brought to their notice.

Inevitably there will be some degree of ***withdrawal*** from social occasions (as we have seen in the Emotional Dimension) for fear of becoming upset or of upsetting others. Friends may not be keen to invite one person when they have always invited two. If a bereaved person does attend social functions, how do they respond in a group now that they are alone?

An elderly mother of several grown-up children declined all offers of contact from her family for several months after her husband died. No matter how her children tried to encourage her, she would not go to their homes at weekends or for meals. The children were extremely worried about their mother's isolation, but after some time she gradually began to accept their invitations once more. When the family were back into their routine of visiting each other and having their mother included, she wrote and thanked them for their concern but explained that nothing they could have done would have helped; she was a sensible woman and needed to be alone with her grief until she was able to handle it properly in her family's presence.

After a major loss, some people may wish to dispose of all reminders of the deceased. Counsellors should note if photographs disappear from places where they were before, or if there are no photographs of the deceased around the house. Photographs may be used as a good tool to help the bereaved come to terms with the loss and help to form a balanced picture of the deceased and the former relationship. ***Avoidance*** of reality can lead to distorted or delayed grief and should be tackled by the counsellor in a sensitive manner. The opposite to avoidance is when people ***idealise*** the deceased and it has been known for the bereaved to develop some sort of shrine to the dead person. Parents who lose young children may preserve the child's bedroom and find it difficult to change it for fear of losing the memory. Both these facets of behaviour are not abnormal, but if they persist for a long term the counsellor should begin to deal with the behaviour before it becomes obsessive. To assist someone like this to live without the deceased can be difficult, but counsellors should try to help by using a problem-solving approach, i.e. looking at what is stopping progress through the grief and how clients can be motivated to use their abilities to make decisions to resolve them.

A bereaved person may ***adopt the traits*** of the deceased and start to take on mannerisms which the dead person displayed. This may change their behaviour and it can suddenly seem inappropriate to others, especially their close relatives.

The bereaved may still lay the table for two, expecting the deceased to return from work. This represents a habitual pattern which may not be abandoned immediately after a loss.

All the behaviours described above are normal patterns which may be displayed following a loss. Although the behaviours may seem strange and disturbing to others, they are usually only episodes which will lead eventually to changed behaviour appropriate to the changed situation. Inappropriate behaviour and habits need to be worked through before reorganisation of lifestyle can be accomplished.

For a counsellor to help, we need to encourage the client to look towards a reorganised behaviour and lifestyle with the minimum of disruption; then we need to help the client evaluate the effectiveness of the new behaviour. In this way we will hope to lower distress, resolve problems and allow the client to perceive that on-going coping is possible, thus reducing the impact of the crisis.

Note:- It should now be obvious how all these Dimensions inter-connect; it is true that most of the Dimensions overlap in reality when we are dealing with the global concept of the person.

Social Dimension

The social moment of death has great significance. It can lead to a redistribution of power and wealth. It requires a reorganisation of the fabric of the family and tends to be the occasion for social ritual to acknowledge the event, i.e. the funeral and the mourning period. These rituals vary from culture to culture and there are also social class differences and individual differences.

I do not propose to detail here all the cultural differences relevant to loss, but we should be aware that they do exist and a knowledge of cultural rituals may help counsellors if they are dealing with certain ethnic families.

The absence of concrete social prescription for bereavement behaviour makes it difficult to anticipate how other people will react, and it confuses the bereaved about how they should act. However, a sense of grief is inevitable and there will be a certain amount of ***loneliness.*** A person may move from being dependent to independent because of the broken attachment bond with a loved one. This leads to change in role and status and disorganised family structure. Differences will occur in power, roles, duties and responsibilities and this may cause family conflict. The bereaved may not be aware of all the roles played by the deceased until then.

Society's attitude to death may lead to segregation from friends, due to the change in status and new financial demands. The bereaved will need to examine what function they fulfilled before the loss and how they will fulfil it now under the changed circumstances. This may lead to ***uncertainty*** and perhaps embarrassment. ***Sorrow*** and ***disappointment*** may well be mixed with anger, guilt and ***anxiety.***

Loneliness and isolation are feelings often expressed by the bereaved, especially by those who have lost a spouse or were used to a day-to-day relationship. Although people may accept the fact that they feel lonely, they may self-induce isolation for the reasons mentioned earlier, e.g. fear of reactions from others and not knowing how to behave themselves towards others. This can lead to segregation from family and friends and compound the isolation.

New relationships may be difficult to make due to difficulties with ***emotional withdrawal,*** again not helping the problem. The counsellor can help the bereaved realise that, although the deceased may never be replaced, it is permissible to fill their place with new and different relationships. For new relationships to succeed, the bereaved will have to be accepted, recognised and appreciated as persons for their own attributes. This can help the bereaved adjust to the changes which will take place in their social life and lead to some independence.

To help people at this time we need to allow them, at first, to come to terms with being alone. They may need help in making both new relationships and the appropriate changes in everyday roles and status. Time is needed to establish their independence, and family conflict may need to be resolved before the new family structure can be accommodated. Even at this time, the bereaved may need to put others at ease and to help them feel comfortable about their loss.

Practical Dimension

Adjusting to changed circumstances and a new role and status means different things to different people, depending on what the previous relation was and who assumed what roles.

Undoubtedly there will be practical issues to be considered at the time of a bereavement. The funeral will have to be organised. We have noted how important it is to talk about one's feelings for the deceased and the funeral is an ideal opportunity for this to happen, despite the tendency for all who attend to ***over-idealise*** the deceased. However, it may have the effect of providing a social network of support for the bereaved, and this kind of support can be helpful for eliminating some of the ***social isolation*** mentioned earlier. It should not be forgotten that immediately after a loss the bereaved may be ***confused*** and ***numb*** and may not appreciate the impact of the funeral rite at this time.

Arrangements may need to be made for child care. Domestic arrangements will alter and financial and employment problems may arise.

Sometimes it will seem easier to do things for the bereaved rather than simply to listen to them and share in their experience. However, the listening and sharing are necessary precursors to encouraging them to do things for themselves, thus increasing self-worth and independence.

If the loss is an amputation leading to a disability, we should remember not to rely on practical help alone and ignore the other Dimensions which will also be affected by the loss.

Feelings of ***helplessness*** and ***anxiety*** are common shortly after a loss, until someone is able to realise their abilities and sort out their new position and responsibilities. At this time family members may over-protect the bereaved and stall progress through the adapting period. We should allow and encourage people to do what they can for themselves.

As good judgment may be difficult to exercise after a significant loss, it is prudent to discourage major life-changing decisions until the person has returned to some sort of equilibrium. It is advisable to work through grief where things are familiar, rather than selling a house and moving to an unknown area. Major decisions, if made in haste for the wrong reasons, may well be regretted later, thus adding to the sense of grief.

Although a slow process, the majority of people who have suffered a major loss do eventually adapt to the practical demands of daily living.

Summary

All the preceding Dimensions are only a useful guide to the different stages which people may pass through during the mourning process. They are not clear cut and it should be remembered that not everyone will pass through every phase in the same sequence, at the same pace or with equal ease. However, they do provide us with a framework of how people may reassess their world and themselves following a major loss.

Having read through the Dimensions, remember that they all represent ***normal grief*** reactions and feelings and that there is nothing pathological about any of them. Nevertheless, feelings which continue for abnormally long periods of time and in excessive intensity may lead to complications in the grieving process. Counsellors will need to know more than this book allows if they are to deal with complicated mourning.

The reason for defining the characteristics of normal grief reaction is to show the wide variety of behaviour and experiences associated with loss. All the reactions may vary in time span and intensity from person to person depending on their vulnerability to change and, of course, the events surrounding the loss.

A wife who has watched her husband suffer a long terminal illness in hospital may well react differently when her husband dies to a mother who suddenly loses her teenage son in a road traffic accident. Was there some advance warning or was the death unexpected?

For some people, grief is an extremely intense experience, while for others it is rather moderate. For some people, grief begins at the time they hear of the loss, while for others the experience may be delayed. In some cases, grief goes on for a relatively short period, while in others it may go on for years.

It is essential for counsellors to recognise and understand this to enable them to give reassurance to people who are disturbed by their own reaction, especially in the case of a first significant loss.

We need not over-protect the client; they need to realise what is happening and why. They need to examine who they are and what they are in order to accept and adapt to a new role.

Counsellors do not necessarily give answers; if we ask the right questions to the clients' responses, they will start to work for themselves. If we create meaning, we give choice for growth. "He who has the ***why*** to live will surely find the ***how.***"

Chapter Two

Crisis Events causing Loss Reaction

In the Introduction to this book, I wrote, "The model and method of application presented in this book may be used in bereavement work; however the counselling skills discussed may also be used in helping people who have suffered any major loss".

It is not possible to discuss every conceivable loss situation but it is worth looking at and thinking about some common forms of crises other than bereavement. There are similarities in each situation but it does not follow that every crisis requires the same handling by a counsellor, although the Dimensions of Adjustment should be looked at to test out the overall progress of the client.

Miscarriage, stillbirth and abortion

When a baby is born, people send flowers, cards and congratulations; it is such a joyful occasion. Thus, when a baby dies, the shock is particularly great.

There are many similarities between the reactions to a stillbirth and the reactions to a spontaneous abortion. If the pregnancy is a planned one, and the couple have been looking forward to the birth of a baby, then the distinction between stillbirth and spontaneous abortion is an academic one. What is important to them is the loss of the baby they were expecting. Even if the pregnancy was not planned, we cannot assume that the child was not wanted and that there is no sense of loss for the parents.

The parents of a stillborn child or of a baby who has died soon after birth may feel very ***alone.*** The first question they may ask is "Why?" Often the doctors and midwives will not know. Even a post-mortem may not provide a clear answer.

It is natural for the parents to wonder if the tragedy could have been avoided. They may ***blame*** themselves or the hospital staff and feel "they could have done something". It could help for the parents to talk to one of the doctors or a midwife and ask all the questions which are in their mind.

The question may arise about whether the parents should see and hold their dead baby. This is not an easy decision and it may seem strange to some parents. The experience of holding the baby can help to make him or her a more real person to remember and can help with ***acceptance*** that the death has occurred. Many people do not understand that a stillborn child is a real person to his or her parents and, after looking forward to the birth during the pregnancy, they may be left with feelings of ***emptiness*** and ***bewilderment.***

After a stillbirth or miscarriage, some women feel that somehow they have 'failed' although they may not be able to talk about this with their husbands. Father may feel that nobody understands that this was his child too and may feel that he has to make the arrangements and generally cope while his wife gets all the sympathy. He may feel it is best not to mention the baby to her, but this may be because he himself finds it too painful.

It is important to remember that all these reactions are normal. Each person will grieve in his or her own way, and husbands and wives may express their emotions in different ways and at different times. If they can be helped to share their grief it will become easier for both to bear it.

A dead baby is part of the family life and, if there are already children, the parents will face the problem of coping with them and explaining to them what has happened.

Older siblings need to be helped at this time. Children need to be told as much of the truth as possible. For some months they have had the promise of a new brother or sister and are now left with nothing. Like their parents, they will feel ***anger, guilt*** and ***grief,*** and they will need careful help to express this in order to pass through their own grieving process.

Losing one baby from a twin birth can also lead to complications. How does one reconcile the joy of having one healthy baby with the despair of losing another?

Even very young children can be affected at this time, although they may not understand what has happened. They may not be able to talk about it and may be very *confused.* They need to be reassured of their parents' love, however difficult this may be for the parents at this time. We need to try to tell them simply what has happened and parents should try to tell them how they feel. At the same time, the children should be encouraged to tell their parents about their feelings too. It is better to answer their questions than to frighten them by leaving them wondering what has happened. Children who felt a bit jealous that the baby was coming may secretly feel that the baby's death was their fault, so a lot of reassurance is needed. Some children may behave badly as a way of showing that they are very upset, or others may hide their feelings until much later.

Sometimes the mother of a stillborn baby feels that she does not want to see too much of her existing child or children. She may remember what they were like as babies and mourn all the more for the baby who will never grow into a child.

It is often remarked that young couples can always have another baby after they have suffered a stillbirth or miscarriage. However, they really need to work through their grief for the baby who has died before contemplating having another.

Most of what has been written in this section about stillbirth and miscarriage can also be applied to many people who plan to have their pregnancies terminated. Some may not show a marked reaction at the time, due to the *relief* of a decision made and the act carried out, but some minor future upset may well trigger off the reactions described above. Women who have had terminations earlier in their life may experience difficulty during a future pregnancy or when they are trying to conceive a planned child.

General surgery

The prospect of surgery is not something which is welcomed by many people, although when pain and discomfort have been experienced for some time the necessity of it may be readily acknowledged. Closely related to the topic of surgical loss is the concept of body image; that is, the picture of our own body as it appears to ourselves.

Depending upon a child's experience, various parts of the body will be seen as good or bad, clean or dirty, mentionable or unmentionable. These attitudes are an integral part of the body image. If this body image is altered by amputation or other surgery, it can lead to grief-like reaction which requires a period of mourning before the trauma is resolved and a new acceptable body image formed. The acceptance of the new image by other people is also important.

Hysterectomy

Varied responses are to be found in women who undergo a hysterectomy operation. Much depends on the age of the woman, her physical and mental health and her relationship if she is married.

The most commonly experienced loss is that which results from the knowledge that she can no longer conceive and bear children. When the possibility of conception is removed, together with hormonal changes, impotency may result. Associated with the loss of libido can be ***insomnia*** and ***lethargy.*** If there has been tension in the marriage, the operation may become the focus of marital disharmony and the ending of sexual relationships.

The feelings of loss associated with a hysterectomy operation do not always lead to severe grief reactions as there are many women who have a known malignancy and are glad to have the operation; they may think that they "will feel better". There are also many who look forward to a new lease of life in which they can enjoy their marriage without any fear of pregnancy.

Mastectomy

Apart from the actual loss of a breast, many patients may experience feelings of mutilation which can be expressed as a loss of attractiveness or femininity . These feelings can be further complicated by fears of malignancy and frequent searching of the other breast for lumps. Patients may appear not to want immediately to consider or discuss prosthesis on the grounds that they fear they "will not live long enough to wear it".

The extent of the grief reaction following a mastectomy may be related to the importance the patient and her family place on busts and the extent to which the patient is reassured that she is still a worthwhile person. Her husband can be a leading figure in providing such reassurance.

The primary stages of ***shock*** and ***disbelief*** may occur at the time of discovery of a lump in the breast. Telling them that the diagnosis may lead to the removal of the breast does not always mean that they accept the fact that it will be removed. The mixture of feelings which may be experienced can vary from ***relief*** that the growth will be removed, to ***resentment*** at being disfigured. These feelings may well be directed at the hospital or the family for allowing it to happen.

Colostomy

The ability to control the bladder and the bowel is a very important step in the development of a child. Many mothers see the end of nappies as a great milestone. To lose this ability has far-reaching effects on an adult person.

The first reaction for many patients when they see their stoma is one of revulsion and, again, a feeling of mutilation. They may become very quiet and ***withdrawn*** and want nothing to do with it, leaving it all to the nursing staff. This reaction may be seen as similar to the ***shock*** and ***disbelief*** in normal grieving.

The inability to accept the permanence of the stoma is often shown by the patient commenting "when will it heal?" or "it seems unnatural handling my own waste". This comment may reflect the patient's past inability to come to terms with their own anatomy and bodily functions, and those who have found toilet habits distasteful tend to suffer more.

Later, when the reality sinks in, the patient will become aware of the mechanics of the stoma and may express fears of smell, accident and giving offence to others. This may lead to problems of ***social isolation, loss of dignity*** and ***acceptability*** to others.

Loss of limb

One of the most obvious forms of loss resulting from surgery is that which follows the amputation of a limb. It seems certain that most patients who have a limb amputated are going to experience both psychological and social problems. To say a patient is feeling 'low' after such an operation can imply a short-term transitory problem, but to say a patient is 'grieving' over the loss of an arm, which would include periods of **depression**, implies the need for a much longer period for adjustment.

The problems experienced by a patient will depend on the limb that is lost, the extent of the amputation and the patient's reaction to previous experiences of loss in his life. The disability may range from complete immobility to the need to acquire new skills and a new lifestyle with an artificial limb. Some patients will cope well, while others will have to ***unlearn old habits*** and for whom ***readjustment*** may be a long and painful process.

An amputee may mourn the loss of a lifestyle and activities as well as the limb itself. These may include a job or sporting activities which required the presence of sound limbs. I remember a man of 80 years old who played football as a young man, but who had not played for 50 years or so. After the amputation of a leg, he complained bitterly that he would no longer be able to play football.

Amputees may display a strong preoccupation with thoughts of the lost limb, sometimes with clear visual images. These thoughts may be accompanied by a strange sense of its physical presence and patients may 'feel' sensations in the lost limb for some time after the amputation. The problems created by the 'phantom limb' may give the patient a reason to ***withdraw*** from responsibilities and social gatherings. Feelings of ***uselessness*** can often be associated with a persistent preoccupation with a phantom limb.

The ***sorrow*** which is displayed by a patient who has lost a limb may not wholly be for the limb itself, but more for the lifestyle, self-image and role in the world which has now been lost. Again, the patient's concept of self-image is an important factor to consider.

The loss associated with amputation may appear to be the same for several patients, but the significance of the loss will vary from person to person.

It is wise, in cases of surgical loss, for some anticipatory counselling to be given, where that is possible, to enable the patient to begin building up a realistic picture of the new life before the old one is destroyed.

Loss of vision

Blindness can arise out of injury, disease or as a result of the ageing process. The onset may be gradual or sudden and the loss may be partial or total. Sudden loss of total vision may cause enormous shock.

The initial reaction to loss of sight may make a person ***immobile*** and ***depressed.*** The person may also be preoccupied with the total ***dependency*** which they feel and the loss of individual freedom. After the initial feelings have subsided, a healthy person may well be concerned with ***economic*** loss and reorganisation of lifestyle and habits.

The rehabilitation process of a person who has experienced loss of vision should aim at restoring as much independence as possible and reintegrating them back into social occasions, thus minimising the effects of ***social isolation*** and ***dependence.*** The ease with which this task may be accomplished will depend on the willingness of the person to be rehabilitated, his or her age and the extent of the visual loss.

Loss of hearing

Gradual loss of hearing may mean that the person is not really aware of what is happening. This may lead to accusations that other people are always mumbling. As deafness progresses, it can lead to feelings of ***isolation, dejection*** and ***distrust*** of those around. Some people may become quite ***angry*** if it is suggested that their hearing is failing; this may infer that they are ageing and they may not wish to acknowledge the fact.

The extent to which a person adjusts to loss of hearing depends on the individual's personality. Reactions may vary from ***denial*** and ***withdrawal*** to concentrating on other physical symptoms and on exploitation of the disability (e.g. 'convenient deafness').

In an adult, as loss of hearing has little effect on already developed speech and mobility, one may expect a fairly good readjustment to the loss of hearing. However, in a young child the results will depend on the age at which the disability occurs and whether there are associated problems of speech development, school and social functioning.

As we should not assume that all blind people are deaf, and raise our voices when talking to them, neither should we assume that all deaf people are incapable of speech.

Fostering and reception into care

If a child is separated from his parents and taken into care, the occasion does not simply mean a change of address for that child. One needs to consider the circumstances of the event;

reactions to a well-planned short-term fostering while a mother is ill in hospital may be quite different from the reactions when it is an abrupt emergency reception into local authority care because, for example, there are suspicions of child abuse, or the parents have perished in a road accident .

The extent to which children grieve over separation from their parents is often not appreciated. For the child, separation from parents is fraught with emotions of ***fear, apprehension, anger, despair*** and ***guilt,*** which may be expressed in many facets of difficult behaviour. Some children's energies may be bent on getting back to their parents, while others may assume that their home has broken up because of their bad behaviour and that they have been taken away as a punishment.

A child's previous experience has led him to expect certain things. Now none of these occur and the ***habitual patterns*** he is accustomed to are interrupted and internal psychological chaos takes over. However, the individual effects of separation on a child from his parents depend very much on the child's state before separation and the conditions when separated.

Parents will also find separation from their children disturbing. They will feel ***threatened*** and frightened of the consequences for their children. They may be ***jealous*** of the foster parents, refuse to visit and leave the children in a turmoil of conflicting loyalties.

Children should be included in the plans made for them and helped to understand the reasons why they are made. One explanation alone may not be enough. The truth which is explained to a child one day may be misconstrued the next by the child's fantasies and ***longing*** for his natural parents. The matter needs to be talked over often and all the child's misconceptions dealt with sympathetically. The child's parents, if possible, should be included in this task.

Retirement

Think for a moment about retirement and what it could mean to you. Look at it in a negative way. There could be an immediate ***loss of self-respect*** at becoming an old-age pensioner and no longer of use to society - a second class citizen. What will the future hold when we retire - inevitable poor health, loss of mobility, inability for self-care leading to entry into a nursing home or old people's home or even a long-term hospital bed. If this happens, all our life will be left behind. Financially we will no longer be bringing in a salary or wage but have to accustom ourselves to the ***lower income*** of our pension. This may well curtail our social activities and hobbies and stop us taking holidays as we used to, or we may not be able to afford to run the car. We may ***lose contact*** with our colleagues and workmates and our social network could well diminish. We shall be at home more, so how will that interfere with our spouse's routine? It could lead to a strained relationship. We could go on and on listing the negative attributes of retirement. If we combine all these negative feelings we may well begin to wonder what reason there is to get up in the morning.

Redundancy and unemployment

It is a sad fact that many people are unaware of the extent of current unemployment and do not realise how even the traditionally 'safe' trades and professions have suffered badly. Long-term unemployment has become a feature for workers of all ages and types. It is not unusual, however, to hear redundant workers state that, with their experience and qualifications, it will not be difficult for them to find another job ***(disbelief)***. By the time they realise just how difficult it is going to be, they may have left the company and are therefore unable to get the counselling support which a skilled personnel manager might have given.

We need to consider how continuing unemployment will affect the whole person, his family and their way of life. How do the unemployed perceive themselves? What will be the financial repercussions of continuing unemployment? There is also the understandable tendency for the longer-term unemployed people to shorten their horizons, ceasing to plan for the future and living instead from one giro cheque to another.

When informed of impending redundancy, many individuals believe that a mistake has been made or that everything will be sorted out before the redundancy takes effect. This ***denial*** often shows in working harder and being very busy as the time for leaving approaches.

For the first few months of unemployment, many individuals actively and constantly seek work. It is often a period of intense activity. As rejection letters mount up, ***boredom, frustration*** and the fear of further ***rejection*** overtake determination, and the job search activity diminishes. Constant rejection is demoralising, particularly with its attendant feelings of ***bitterness, anger, frustration and confusion.*** The long-term effects of continual rejection can be very debilitating, similar to the debilitating effects of constant pain or illness. Eventually, many individuals will withdraw from making job applications to escape still further rejection.

Individuals must be helped to accept their new unemployed identity before they can go on and do something else. For some, downward mobility is a feature of protracted unemployment, and jobs which previously would have been decried may now be accepted. Consequently many may have to re-enter the labour market in a poorly paid unskilled capacity or seek retraining.

The lack of disposable income and the reality of life in the poverty trap is one of the most damaging and demoralising aspects of daily life for the long-term unemployed. Spells of short-term unemployment may be coped with financially by dipping into reserves, but as unemployment lengthens, problems may arise when the reserves have gone and even replacing worn-out shoes may become a financial and family crisis.

The connection between unemployment and ill-health is well documented. Research has shown a substantial increase among the unemployed of stress-related disorders, e.g. coronary problems, hypertension and ulcers, together with psychosomatic illnesses. Loss of employment may also include the loss of one's source of exercise, and this also has repercussions on the general health of an individual.

Family problems are likely to increase as the period of unemployment lengthens. Gender stereotypes are severely threatened as men are deprived of their 'breadwinner' status and may attempt to usurp the 'homemaker' role usually occupied by women. This, when combined with the increased amounts of time which partners spend together at home, can exacerbate family tensions and generate ***anger, resentment*** and ***hostility.*** A renegotiation of roles is often necessary, but it tends to be neglected due to financial pressures.

Unemployment is both an individual and a family problem; the ***frustration*** and ***despair*** of the individual can eventually drive the family apart. Often family relationships suffer as unemployed individuals work out their antagonisms on their partners and children.

As desperation increases, some people can be helped before it leads to apathetic resignation. They may be helped to realise that there are no jobs for them as they are. With an ability to look at their situation more realistically and rationally, they may accept that this is the way things are and their minds can then focus on alternatives. Retraining might be an answer, part-time work considered, self-employment looked at more seriously or some voluntary activity undertaken. They may still be fragile psychologically and will find themselves swamped by feelings of ***hopelessness*** and ***despair*** when things go wrong, but at least they have taken the first steps along the only road which offers them hope for the future. Unemployment can become a busy time again.

Separation and divorce

Being rejected in love, separation and divorce each incurs grief reactions to the loss which affects the daily lives of those involved. It can lead to financial hardship and the need for a total reorganisation of lifestyle, coupled with emotional and psychological readjustment. Both parents and children need to be considered at this time. Children especially will experience a great sense of loss. They may experience feelings of ***emptiness, tearfulness, lack of concentration*** and ***fatigue,*** and ***nightmares*** are not uncommon. All of these are symptoms of mourning. This sense of loss may coincide with adolescent feelings of outgrowing the family. If both these feelings merge, their grief will be magnified; the family is no longer available to them because of one parent's departure and they have nothing to rely on as they make their first tentative venture outside the 'nest'.

The psychological and social obstacles which confront children and their divorcing parents are formidable and the road to stability is much longer than many people realise. Divorce is not a single event; it is a chain of events, a series of legal, social, psychological, economic and sexual changes strung complexly together and extended over time. Thus separating the strands of the 'mess' (see page 64) is essential if counsellors are to help people successfully through such a situation.

We should not forget that this is not the total sum of loss situations - think about ***imprisonment*** or ***going into a home for the elderly*** - there are numerous other situations in which major loss is incurred. Some amount of grief and mourning occurs in all kinds of life-situations. Fairly ordinary changes, such as moving to a new house, involves some sorrow at losing familiar surroundings or the closeness of friends. Changing jobs can allow us to experience sadness at parting from our colleagues. Every move forward that we make in life may provide us with pleasure but may also mean leaving something or someone behind. These events lead to the growth of individuals and help us face the future life-crises that we can expect to encounter.

Chapter Three

Practical Interviewing Techniques

Introduction

Good interviewing contains a large element of individual style. This means that there is no one best way to interview; it is not a mechanical exercise, or at least it should not be. What works well for one interviewer may not work so well for another - and we all have our 'off days'!

However, improvement is possible. Our aim should be improvement rather than perfection. Most social workers and counsellors are already relatively good at some interviewing skills, but could probably improve their range of skills and so have more options.

Improving interviewing techniques involves some sense of awkwardness, but acquiring skills goes with practice. This is true with sport, driving or any other activity; soon they become second nature - unfortunately the same applies to wrong skills.

If we start by exploring a problem with a client, we can slow down the process of trying to solve it. If we have maximum information about a problem, effective action is more likely. We need to establish a good relationship with clients and this is intended to help them explore what they want to say and what they feel about the difficulties in their lives.

Exploring a problem helps the interviewer and the client clarify the information given. Saying something out loud helps to test out how true it is and can start clients thinking about their own determination to solve their problems. We should try to keep the focus on the clients to check out their and our understanding of the problem. Don't think "I know how they feel"; try to think "What does this mean to them?".

If there are multiple problems - and usually there is more than one - it is appropriate to concentrate on one problem at a time and try to resolve it before we get bogged down with too much confusing information. We should try to encourage clients to decide which problem is most important to them. For example, we could ask: "which of these aspects would you like to talk about first", or "of all these, the one that stands out as worrying you most is...".

The idea here is that once a relatively trusting relationship has been established and once clients have given a certain amount of information, it is desirable to help them explore one problem or aspect of a problem more thoroughly. If not, there is a danger of going round in circles and avoiding the main issues.

Active listening

When interviewing, if we get the correct facts, this will help build a foundation for our initial assessment. It is well to remember that, if we retain wrong information or forget important facts, trust will be difficult to establish and clients will not be keen to open up and give more information if they feel it is not being heard or if it is being distorted. We need to ***listen actively.***

Active listening can be practised in pairs with a colleague or partner. For five minutes one person tells the other details about themselves, e.g. where they were born, married or single, any children, where they work, etc., giving as many facts as possible. The person listening does not speak but merely ***attends*** and tries to retain all the facts being related.

The two then change places and the person who has been talking now becomes the listener, and vice versa.

There have now been two exchanges of information. The first listener should now relay back to the first speaker all the facts which can be remembered. When they have done this, the first speaker should comment on whether it was correct, was anything left out, were any mistakes made, and so on. Repeat the exercise again with the second listener relaying back factual information to the second speaker. Again comments are received back on the quality of the retention of facts.

This exercise is useful on courses as an initial way of giving group information and allowing people to get to know each other. After two people have paired off and exchanged information, the group can come back together and each person introduce the partner to the group. Discussion may follow about how easy or difficult the group found the exercise.

There are two objectives to this exercise:-

- It will introduce the members of the group to each other, and the group will start to support itself by the sharing of personal information. It also facilitates the correcting of a colleague if wrong information is given about another. Hopefully, rapport will start to be established in the group and the leader will try to create a safe environment for people to disagree and discuss. Some members of the group will be shy and reserved and may find this exercise difficult; therefore it is up to the leader to help the person 'open up' and be supported by the group.
- This exercise will also help counsellors become aware of how much factual information they are able to retain in one session. If they get facts right, this will help build a relationship with their client. If they get facts wrong, their assessments will also be incorrect and therefore their short, medium and long-term aims for the client will also be wrong and may need to be changed soon after work with the clients begins.

By listening actively we shall also begin to understand how the client is feeling.

Reflective listening and paraphrasing

Reflective listening encourages the client to continue talking, as it shows *acceptance* of the client's feelings which, at this time, is all-important. We need to show people that they are not alone, or odd, because of the strange feelings they are experiencing. Reflecting someone's feelings back to them also shows ***empathy,*** so try using a different but similar word or phrase to show your understanding of how they are feeling. For example, the client may say "I felt such a fool at the time". We could reflect "That must have been uncomfortable". Or the client may say "I was furious with them", and we could reflect "It must have been upsetting".

This exercise may be practised in pairs once again. One person thinks of a recent situation which has aroused some kind of feeling. Here are some examples to use: try to imagine

a) You were told off at work today for something that was not your fault.

b) You were preparing a meal for special friends and everything went wrong.

c) You are on your way to help a friend in distress and the car breaks down.

d) Your daughter comes home to say she has been bullied at school.

e) A letter from school informs you that your son has been truanting for over two weeks.

f) Your husband informs you he has been made redundant.

g) You recently saw a wonderful film and you are explaining to a friend how much you enjoyed it.

h) You return from work to find your house has been burgled.

i) You are an unemployed, single mother and the Electricity Board has informed you that they will cut off the supply in seven days.

The speaker describes the situation briefly to the other person saying how he or she *felt.* The person listening ***reflects*** this feeling back to the person relating the event to try to show ***empathy.*** This time there is no need to listen for details but rather concentrate on the feelings being expressed and the depth of that feeling, e.g.

Teller - "It really made me laugh".

Listener - "Sounds like a funny situation".

In this way the feeling experienced is reflected back by using a different but similar word or phrase showing the teller that you are in tune with the situation and aware of how it made them feel. Hearing this the teller will either correct you if you are wrong, and go on to elaborate more, or agree and again explain more. The reflection or paraphrase, if possible, should be an encouragement for the teller to 'open up' and feel at ease; i.e. "Here is someone who understands how I feel/felt".

When both persons in the pair have had their feelings reflected back in an appropriate way, the group can reform in a circle. Again, a situation is spoken of by one person and the person on the left reflects back the feeling using a different word or phrase. If the word or phrase is inappropriate, the group can help out by finding a more suitable word or phrase to describe the feeling and its depth or intensity; e.g. if the client says "I was furious", the counsellor might reply "It must have been upsetting". This is a far more appropriate response than "You were angry" as the latter does not 'encourage' the client to elaborate, although it may confirm the feeling. The object of the exercise is to allow the client to see that you understand and it is safe to go on. You are being receptive and letting them know this by reflecting that you are aware of their feelings and interested in what they are telling you.

Go on round the group so that everyone has a chance to practise, for practising techniques is so important in developing skills.

The main objective of this session is to let clients know that you are listening and understanding. If clients have their feelings reflected in an appropriate way, it will not hinder their flow of conversation; as they realise that the counsellor is 'with them', they will feel encouraged to go on. However, if the reflection is not correct, they may elaborate to allow you to get it right, or they may shut off because you "just don't understand". However, when reflection and paraphrasing is correct, it continues to allow clients to open up, as they will find the listener concerned, comforting and aware of their situation.

Open and closed questions

It cannot be stated too often that, as counsellors, we need to encourage clients to talk freely. If they have recently been bereaved, they may not feel like opening up to a stranger, so it may be difficult to elicit the information we need to work on the Dimensions of Adjustment model discussed in the earlier part of this book.

Closed questions are those which gain a short, sharp answer with no details; e.g. "How are you?" - o.k.; "Are you eating?" - yes; "Is money a problem?" - of course. We need to avoid questions which receive such answers and, instead, develop a repertoire of ***open questions*** which bring forth more detail.

Closed questions are appropriate if we wish to check out a fact or a piece of information; e.g. "How old is she?" or "Did it happen six or nine days ago?".

Instead of asking "Is money a problem?', to which the reply could be "yes" or "no", we may say "How has your financial situation changed?". Or, instead of asking "Are you sleeping well?", which again could elicit another "yes" or "no", we may say "How do you get your rest?".

Open questions elicit more information, without sounding like interrogation.

Questions starting with *when, what, how or where* open up the question as well as showing that we are interested in the reply and also in a certain area of the client's adjustment. When we are interviewing bereaved clients, we should be thinking of the

Dimensions described in Chapter 1, i.e. Mental, Physical, Emotional, Behavioural, Social and Practical, so that our assessment covers all these Dimensions.

At specific interviews we can home in on certain Dimensions which are causing problems or blocks if we are following the path of the client's adjustment within each Dimension, and if we feel this particular area needs further examination.

Remember - can a question be answered with a "Yes" or "No"? - then it is ***closed.*** Does it elicit more information than just a "Yes" or "No"? - then it is ***open.*** Here are a few examples of relevant questions relating to the Dimensions of Adjustment.

Mental/Spiritual

Closed: Do you feel suicidal?
Open: How does the future look?

Practical/Behavioural

Closed: Are you eating?
Open: How are you managing your food?

Mental/Emotional

Closed: Are you unhappy?
Open: When are the worst moments?

Practical/Social

Closed: Are you managing the children?
Open: When do the children seem most difficult?
or: How have the children changed since they lost their father?

Physical

Closed: Have you seen the Doctor about your back pain?
Open: When did the pains start?

From the above few examples we should now be able to see how these exercises and techniques can be a useful tool to employ together with the Dimensions of Adjustment model.

General and specific questions

If a counsellor is looking at one Dimension, or wishes to home in on a client's problem in this area, we need again to put the client at ease about talking on this area before they may freely do so. The client may be blocking or find it difficult to explain, so we need to help unblock them.

By making a *general* comment which is acceptable, we can then become *specific* about the person's own experience. For example, a recently widowed woman is looking pale and thin, complaining of pains and looking washed out. We want to know, in the Practical and Physical Dimensions, whether she is eating properly. Our instincts feel she probably is not, but does she realise that lack of food may be the reason for her poor physical condition? To ask her "Are you eating well?" is silly; it is obvious she is not, but she could well say "Yes". A *general* comment could be "Some people find it difficult shopping and cooking for one". Here the counsellor is *empathising* with an obvious difficulty but not actually saying "*You* are having difficulty!". Hopefully this general comment allows the client to agree; if she agrees and knows this to be correct, the counsellor can become *specific* and say "How are you managing your food?". This is *specific* and *open.*

Or, if the client is crying a lot, the counsellor may make a *general* comment such as "Bereavement is a sad time for those who are left". This shows *empathy* and helps the client see that she is not alone with this feeling. Again, if she agrees, the counsellor may become *specific* and ask "When are your worst moments?". Once more this is *specific* and *open* and allows the client to know that the counsellor understands there are going to be bad times and is interested enough to want to hear about them.

This technique may also be termed Indirect and Direct Questioning. Here are a few more examples indicating the relevant Dimensions with which they may be associated.

Emotional

General: Bereavement is a sad time.
Specific: When do you cry most?

Behavioural

General: A lot of people don't want to leave the house at a time like this.
Specific: How often do you go out?

Social/Behavioural

General: Children often play up when one parent dies.
Specific: Are your children being a handful?

Social

General: Families can often provide comfort in times of trouble.
Specific: Will your relatives come to see how you are?

Mental/Intellectual

General: It is not unusual for a bereaved person to forget that someone is dead.
Specific: Do you still talk to him?

Mental/Spiritual

General: Many people can't think ahead at this time.
Specific: How do you see the future?

All through our interviews we are looking to form a continuous assessment of a bereaved person's passage through the Dimensions of Adjustment described earlier. Although counsellors are not there to give decisions, they are there to prompt and encourage clients to work through their problems. Some clients may not feel that they have problems, so we have to be sensitive with our questioning and not allow the client to block further because "the counsellor does not understand how I feel". Open, closed, general and specific questioning, if used appropriately, relays to the client our concern and understanding; it allows them to talk through and examine the process and to become aware. They will begin to understand what is happening and why, and what needs to be done to resolve the state they are in.

Counsellors can help speed the process of adjustment if, and only if, they themselves are aware of what stage the client is at. To assess this stage correctly, we need true information, gained from the client of their own free will, and given in a safe environment. Clients may only give information to someone they trust, who understands and who is sensitive about a delicate, disturbing situation. We also need to gain the maximum of information without making clients feel interrogated. We need to make it easy for them to indicate to us where they are in their adjustment in all the Dimensions.

Summary

We have looked at several techniques which can be used when interviewing in a counselling situation. Although it may appear on paper that we have only done three basic things - active listening, reflective listening and questioning - we have in fact covered many more aspects of counselling skills.

With ***active listening,*** we are sharing experiences and reporting back. We are thinking about retention of facts and getting them correct and, at the same time, using this information for future work with the client. We are assessing the client's problems from the very beginning of contact.

With ***reflective listening,*** we are trying to show empathy and get closer to the client to begin to form a relationship. We are establishing trust and allowing the client to know that we are a safe person to talk to. As counsellors, we are assessing the depth of feelings to see what needs to be done to help the client move on. At the same time, we should be thinking about how we are going to help the client do this. We are showing acceptance of their situation and helping them to look to the future and the changes this may bring. Remember, we are assessing for a person to move to the restoration of functional ability and therefore we are planning long-term aims from the early stages of our contact. If clients realise that we are making long-term aims, this will help them look to the future also and will bring hope to what may seem a hopeless situation.

With *questioning skills,* we are again helping the client to move on. We are attempting to remove blocks while gaining information on particular Dimensions to use in our assessments. With open and specific questioning we are showing our interest and concern. This is the basis for the client's trust in us, so that the client can share more about their own situation and, in the process, begin to understand its causes and what might be done to alter it.

Hopefully both the client and counsellor are working to a time when the bereaved person can handle the loss appropriately and return to a changed but comfortable way of life.

Chapter Four

Counselling Process & Skills

Introduction

To become a successful counsellor, one needs to know not only the theories, principles and techniques to be employed, but also, and perhaps more importantly, when and how to implement them. Comfortable counselling will only be achieved when one does not have to struggle to sift through the extensive knowledge of theory, principles and techniques for the correct response to a client's dilemma, but when one automatically picks the suitable reaction. This may only be achieved by grasping the theories and understanding their implication and use and continuing to practise in real situations. At first, as with anything new, one may feel clumsy and make mistakes, but, in time, as with learning to drive, one knows instinctively when to break, accelerate or change gear to keep moving at a steady safe pace.

Counselling may be based on the assumption that there is value in the free expression of both painful and pleasant feelings and in the honest examination of conflicts. Helpful relationships offer more than reassurance and the exchange of pleasantries. They are the context in which uncomfortable subjects can be examined and individuals can feel accepted as a whole person, for their badness as well as their goodness. Counselling provides the opportunity for individuals to reflect on the nature of their problems and the options before them. Counselling should be offered and not imposed, so we need some way of establishing whether we should offer it or not.

What follows, in this chapter, is a plan of work which will lead the counsellor, together with the client, to a point where a joint decision can be made about whether counselling should be attempted. If the decision is that it should be attempted, we then move on to the counselling process itself and finally look at how and when the process should end.

In Chapter 1, I emphasised that the stages of the Dimensions of the mourning process should not be taken too literally. However, now, with the counselling process, it should become obvious that the steps which I shall describe here do follow in chronological order. Until one has met the client, achieved a social history, defined and assessed the problem, one cannot move on to actual counselling if, at this time, the counsellor feels it would be beneficial to the client. Obviously individual counsellors may wish to modify my progression in accordance with their own style, but I am confident that this planned approach is useful to follow.

Opening

The beginning of the client/counsellor relationship is an extremely important time. Before we attempt to counsel the bereaved, it is very necessary to look at our own capabilities. What are our own strengths and weaknesses? We need to think about our own feelings in relation to loss. We should be aware of our own feelings of the emotional burden we are taking on and appreciate the limits of our own helplessness and the unique impact of each loss. It is wise to recognise the wide range of reactions which can occur in apparently similar situations.

Feelings of anger and frustration may arise in counsellors if they feel uncomfortable at witnessing the pain of others. This may cause them to cut short their counselling contract, leaving the client with important work undone. We need to be sure we can overcome the fear of loss of control in ourselves when evoking grief in others.

If losses in counsellor's own life are not adequately resolved, these may surface and inhibit or distort the expression of grief by the client. This could lead to over-identification with a similar personal experience; to 'top' the client's experience with one of our own will not help the client at all. A counsellor who has recently lost a spouse through death or divorce may well find it difficult to work with someone who has suffered a similar loss. However, a counsellor's experience with a similar loss may be beneficial if the counsellor has worked through his or her own grief successfully. Even so, there is always a danger that the counsellor will need to deal personally with being emotionally overwhelmed.

At times, counsellors may need to face up to the reality of their own mortality. This may be heightened if they are counselling a client who has lost someone who was similar to the counsellor in terms of sex, age and status.

Counsellors must be sure that they can overcome reserve and embarrassment when talking about painful and personal topics such as death, cancer, sexual relationships, etc.

Some counsellors may take on more clients than they should but find it difficult to admit they have become overloaded. Some may find it hard to withdraw their support at the end of the counselling process and perhaps create dependence rather than independence for their clients.

After all this self-evaluation by the counsellor, it is essential that they know how to seek help for themselves and know where they can go for support.

When counsellors are sure that they know their limitations, where to get their own emotional support and how to reach out for it, they can now begin to establish a relationship with clients.

When a client is referred, don't prejudge information from the referral but do hypothesise about behaviour, sensitivities and possible problem areas for the client. By doing this, we can develop a strategy aimed at maximising the client's comfort and our own efficiency in gathering relevant information.

At the initial interview, introduce yourself, your role and the purpose of the meeting. Think about the seating, distance, tone of voice and speed of questioning. Prepare time to talk without rushing and without interruption. Trying to reach solutions to emotional problems is a mutual responsibility shared by client and counsellor.

Don't be afraid of silences; give the client time to reflect or expand on a topic. Express bewilderment if something appears to be confusing - don't just accept it - and ask the client to go over it again so that you can both clarify the point. For example:- "Let me be sure I understand"; "I'm confused about the last point - can you clarify it"; "I'm getting the impression that you are most upset about...". Make sure you both understand the situation. Be sensitive to both verbal and non-verbal signs of discomfort and reassure the client about their concerns. Try to put them at ease. For example:- "People are often concerned about seeking professional help"; "I'm glad you came - you seem to be very concerned about these problems and this is the first step in doing something about them"; "It takes a great deal of courage to talk about such private matters with someone you don't know". We must try to form a purposeful relationship right from the start.

Getting the case history

I do not believe that we are automatically equipped to be able to discuss such topics as sex, anger, hallucinations, suicide, etc. It requires a concerted effort and practice to be comfortable about such subjects and to communicate this comfort to the client. We can model in this area by being direct and forthright, yet accepting and understanding of the uneasiness involved.

We should ask questions tactfully, not in Spanish Inquisition style. Avoid closed questions. The more sensitive the question, the more sensitive we need to be about the asking.

We will need to employ our active listening, reflective listening and paraphrasing skills to assist the client in giving a detailed case history. We need to know what the client's life was like before the loss, at the time of the loss and since the loss. It is also important to hear what the client says about the future, for this is the time to assess whether the client's mourning process is healthy or not.

Misunderstanding may occur if the client's behaviour does not truly reflect what he or she feels or intends to convey. People who are distressed may not take sufficient care to express their thoughts or feelings clearly. Sometimes they will send double messages or give subtle non-verbal clues to describe their feelings, rather than openly say what they feel. The counsellor is expected to notice them, interpret them accurately and respond to them appropriately. Here again, our reflective listening and paraphrasing skills can be useful for clarification.

Know what you want to ask about and ask concisely. Pick up links the client has made, e.g. "It's like Granny's illness".

Beware - don't open mouth before engaging brain!

Try to get an account of the client's current problems as the client sees them - "Tell me about the problems you have been having".

Give an opportunity for clients to begin with what seems to them to be important. From then on the counsellor can ask more specific questions until the situation becomes clear on all the Dimensional levels.

Each area brought up by the client can be pursued in this way - from general to specific. Use open, direct and indirect questions to gain information and insight into the problem. This will help to clarify the degree or amount of feeling or a behaviour. For example, feeling 'down' may mean tired and unhappy to you or I, but may mean an inability to leave the house and suicidal thoughts to the client. Always stick to the topic - don't avoid painful areas. If you do, try to develop an ability to return to them later.

Perhaps the most important factor to remember about communication is that it is a mutually influencing process. Even when we are seemingly doing nothing, we are communicating and have an effect on the other person. While the client is the one who is saying the words and I, the counsellor, am the one who is receiving the verbal message, I am also a sender of non-verbal messages. These, if noticed by the client, will influence what the client says and how it is said. The client and counsellor will be communicating, in some way, all the time.

At each interview, both the client and counsellor will have an experience that will affect them in some way. The experience can serve to reinforce what is expected, either positively or negatively. It may create doubts about the other's worth and so create mistrust, or it may deepen and strengthen the worth of each, and the trust and closeness between them. What we, as counsellors, must try to do is create a safe atmosphere where we can develop trust and confidence for and in our clients.

Soon we will begin to understand the development of the problem and start to make an assessment of any dangers or immediate crises facing the client. To make this assessment, we need to evaluate the client's emotional response to the difficulties. Try to understand the client's current life situation and how it interacts with the presenting problem. Try to evaluate what the client wants and expects in the way of help with these problems; also, evaluate the client's own coping skills.

Any interview situation can have its problems, so try to plan ahead. Use supervision with a senior, if necessary, particularly if you have difficulty 'thinking on your feet'. Thoughtful preparation can make the difference between a successful treatment plan being established or the client leaving and being uncertain about returning. The initial interview is very important as it can make or break follow-up by the client.

However, ***don't panic!*** Remember, you do not have to answer every question the client asks. Keep in mind that almost everything you say is repairable. If the initial interview is successful and the client returns you will have another opportunity to ask forgotten questions.

Assessment

When the counsellor has achieved maximum information from the client, it is time to summarise the information and start to assess the client's state and the action which needs to be taken.

An ability to think clearly should enable the counsellor to make a brief summary of the client's situation in each of the Dimensions of Adjustment to the loss. This may be done by pulling together common themes displayed by the client in each of the Dimensions. We need to sort out the relevant from the irrelevant information in order to reduce confusion in ourselves and the client and to clarify the problem areas. This will allow a choice to be made about which problems should be tackled first. Remember: "Which of these aspects would you like to talk about first?".

At this time the counsellor may need to be assertive, without being aggressive, to confront the client and deal with any denial. The counsellor's concept of what is a problem may not be the same as the client's perception of his or her troubles. We may need again to summarise and identify the changes which have taken place in the client's life and redefine the problem-solving exercise for both people involved, but it could be the start of building independence in the client and the beginning of restoring a positive concept of the future to increase the client's self-determination for growth.

This time is an opportunity for the counsellor to point out what the client's own abilities are, which will help to raise self-esteem and show the client that we do not intend to do all the work towards restoration of functional ability, but that the client will also need to utilise all his or her strength and capability.

Clients at this stage may now have a clear idea of what would be desirable changes in their lives. They may also know exactly what to do to achieve these. We may find that, having made an assessment, some clients are well able to cope alone without our continued therapeutic intervention, but may simply need monitoring from time to time. We may be able to set goals with them which they are able to accomplish themselves or with the aid of their own social network.

Counsellors may know of an alternative resource in the community, such as a self-help group, which they feel to be more appropriate than intense counselling. If so, the client should be helped to see the significance of this choice. Counsellors may express their own evaluation of such a choice, but in such a way that the client does not feel obligated to accept the choice and "do as the counsellor told me".

Now may be the end of the process which involves a counsellor, or it may not be. Any such decision should be mutually agreed for, if the client does not feel able to cope, the counsellor may encourage regression in the client if contact is broken, thus undoing all the good work done and the progress already made.

Goal setting and counselling contract

If both the client and the counsellor agree that counselling should continue, definite plans need to be made about long-term aims for the client and what will be expected of both people to achieve these aims. We need to consider a plan of work together that is within the client's ability.

I discussed earlier how some clients may seem to get worse before they start to get better. Perhaps we should warn the client of this before counselling begins. It is wise to re-affirm to the client that not talking about something does not prevent the inevitable from happening. It is better to be prepared for something when it occurs because we then may have had the opportunity to think of ways of handling it.

We should now have a good idea of a client's behaviour, and we should use this knowledge to think about aims and goals for them to work toward a healthy resolution of grief. We need to think about whether our goals are too general or too specific and whether they are realistic for the client to meet. If we identify long-term goals, we may well need short-term aims to reach these goals. We must try not to be overwhelmed, or overwhelm the client, with the whole situation. It may be easier, and more comfortable for the client, to break down the overall problem into manageable pieces. If we have skill in logical problem-solving, we will be able to separate the strands of the 'mess' to deal with one problem at a time.

To use an allegory, I remember my Grandmother saving short pieces of string, knotting them together and forming a big ball ready for use at another time. As a 'whole', the ball of string looked like a complicated mess. When string was needed, my Grandmother would unravel the beginning of the ball and methodically untie the knots. Piece by piece she had what she wanted, while still leaving a smaller 'mess' to unravel later when needed. This story may symbolise to the client that if we unravel the largest knot or problem first, the remaining knots or problems will not seem so difficult to undo.

However, we should not give false hope. We should try to allow our clients to come to their own conclusions about problem-solving, rather than tell them how we would do it. What we are doing is giving our clients permission to plan their own future, but being directive to allow them to look ahead. If we can see a change for the good in the future, this will help them begin to see a future for themselves also.

Although I have suggested previously that we should not ignore negative reactions and painful feelings, now is the time to input positives as a reward at the client's breakthrough points. We should acknowledge their determination to accomplish the aims and reach the goals agreed.

It is important, when we have decided that the client needs and wants continued help, to consider who is the best person to offer this help. We may decide that other organisations or agencies are better than ourselves for this kind of work. Loss takes time to heal and we may need to consider whether we can afford the time it may take. Good counselling requires continued support.

We need to be sure that clients want to be helped now, for they may not be ready to accept counselling at this stage. Does the client really believe that counselling will help? The counsellor needs to believe in the benefit and success of grief work and be able to define the counselling role.

Some people deal effectively with grief alone, while others look for help with thoughts, feelings and behaviour which they cannot cope with. Some people will not seek out help directly but will accept the offer of help if they acknowledge they are having difficulty resolving the loss on their own.

A decision about when to start counselling is important. Unless we have known the client before the loss, we should remember that immediately after the loss the client may still be in a state of shock or numbness and not ready to sort out the confusion. There are no set rules about time schedules for counselling. This will have to be decided by the circumstances of the loss and how the client is referred to the counsellor.

Once contact has been established and the client agrees to return regularly, there are practical issues which need to be considered by the counsellor. Where will the counselling sessions be held? Should it be in the office or in the client's home? Again there is no definite answer to this question, but if we are to notice how clients are functioning from day to day it may be helpful to visit them in their own home. To establish their Dimensional Adjustment, first-hand knowledge of their daily routine and environment would be advantageous. Remember the Dimensions where we need to look for clues, such as stress reduction addiction, pills and drink, have photographs been moved and what is the food situation in the home?

When a contract is agreed, perhaps one of the most difficult decisions is how long it should continue. The client may wish to know how many sessions will be needed, so we should be realistic and remember the client's disposition and the long-term goals we have set and agreed.

Certain times in the mourning process will be particularly difficult for the client and our support may be needed at such times as the deceased's birthday, wedding anniversaries or Christmas and, of course, at the first anniversary of the loss. This does not mean that we will counsel regularly for a year, but if regular contact has ceased it may be encouraging to recontact the client around the first anniversary of the loss. Difficult thoughts and feelings may come to the fore at this time and often a client may need extra support.

How often we contact the bereaved depends on the relationship we have established with them and their adjustment advancement. Bear in mind that grief takes time to be resolved and the counsellor needs to realise that contact may stretch over some time even if actual face-to-face contact is not very frequent.

Once clients have accepted a counselling contract, we should remember not to encourage them to depend on us, but to start to allow them to grow towards their own independence.

Working through grief

We should now be able to move on to the actual counselling work. For the purpose of this book, we will now need to move back to Chapter One and the Dimensions of Adjustment for a description of what the work may involve. It has already been suggested that we need to practise theory to become good counsellors; therefore it was necessary to explain the theory of the Dimensions of Adjustment before going on to illustrate how it may be implemented in practice.

Case Study A

Tom, Mary's husband, died on their daughter's tenth birthday while he was having a heart bypass operation. A few weeks after her husband's death, Mary became very friendly with Steve, a business associate. Steve had also been a family friend of Mary and Tom for some years, so it did not seem unreasonable that he should help and support Mary at this time. Throughout the next few months, a relationship developed even though Steve himself was married. A year after Tom's death, almost to the day, Mary became very depressed. Steve left her, as he could not cope with her moods. Mary attempted to overdose with tablets and was taken to hospital. She accepted counselling.

Initially, Mary was extremely emotional, drank a lot and cried most of the time. She was preoccupied with having no future, being a personal failure and saw no purpose to go on (Spiritual Dimension). She also expressed ***anger*** with herself for "pushing Tom into having the operation", and she ***blamed*** herself and the hospital for its failure (Psychological Dimension). After allowing Mary to talk about her life for some time, her past history indicated that she had always been well supported by family, husband and friends. The death of her husband was her first significant loss and she had never been alone before. Her grief for the death of her husband had been submerged for a year due to her relationship with Steve, and surfaced only when she was faced with her daughter's next birthday, which would always be a reminder of Tom's death. Her overdose was precipitated by Steve leaving her - an additional loss.

By indicating to her that there were similar themes recurring in her past life - living with and being supported by parents, living with and being supported by Tom and then living with and being supported by Steve - she was able to acknowledge her feelings of ***loneliness, isolation*** and fear of an unknown future. Life had always been planned by others and now she was unable to look ahead and plan a future without the support of someone very close. She was able to admit that, although she felt she had wanted to die, Mary herself had called the ambulance at the time of her overdose as she was afraid to face death alone.

From the time Mary was able to understand that she needed plans and structure in her life and that she alone had to construct them, she began to think about what she would do at weekends to fill her time. Should she return to work after many years? Which friends could she invite to her home for meals? Gradually she was able to develop a new ***independence, change old habits*** and ***reorganise*** her lifestyle.

When she began to see a new future for herself, she was able to discuss her feelings about being responsible for Tom's death and her preoccupation with "insisting on the operation which killed him". She had had a good marriage for twenty years and thought now of Tom and herself as one person - his decisions were hers and hers were his. Mary needed to realise that they were, in fact, two separate people with individual thoughts and ideas. Through being helped to talk about Tom's capabilities in his business and his management of the household, Mary soon became aware that Tom was a person who could and did make his own decisions. His family had a history of heart disease and he had often mentioned to Mary that he would discuss a bypass operation with his doctor (a matter which, in her upset emotional state, Mary had forgotten). Only after he had discussed it at length and considered all the pros and cons did Tom choose to go ahead with the operation. Mary felt less guilty and blamed the hospital less when she was able to comprehend that she had not influenced Tom, but he had been strong enough to decide about his own treatment in a methodical manner.

Mary continued to be counselled and other Dimensions of her adjustment improved over several months.

Case Study B

Wanda was referred by a Gynaecologist after she had requested a termination of pregnancy which was refused as he could find no legal, social or moral reason for it to be performed.

Wanda, 23 years old, came to live in Britain from Ghana about two years previously when she was to begin a degree course. She had a husband who was studying medicine in Russia. They had been married according to Ghanaan law but had not been through a church ceremony, which they both wanted to have in this country. A year before, Wanda had had an abortion after she was raped. The rape had taken place at her cousin's home while she was babysitting. One of her cousin's friends, who had been drinking, came into the bedroom where she was sleeping with the two children. Wanda said that she was not able to resist as she did not want to wake the children and upset them. She did not report it to the police as the man had threatened to prevent her doing so. When she found she was pregnant, she was advised by her clergyman to seek a termination as the child was a result of rape.

Within the next few months Wanda's husband visited her here and she told him about the rape. Although Wanda and her husband were 'married', the traditional Ghanaan ceremony was performed while he was in Russia and his brother had 'stood in' for him. She had been a virgin before the event and had not had sex with her husband.

Because of the complex range of difficulties Wanda was experiencing, it was essential to 'separate the strands of a mess' and deal with one issue at a time. There were areas of emotional and psychological distress, social and cultural implications, relationship problems, practical problems and spiritual confusion which Wanda needed to examine. After a counselling contract was agreed, Wanda decided to discuss her feelings about the rape and the termination before considering the future relationship with her husband and the forthcoming birth of her baby. Various aspects about the rape and abortion were still causing her confusion.

She felt ***guilty*** and ***blamed*** herself for letting the man into her cousin's house. She said that her religion taught her cleanliness and she now felt unclean and that "God did not want her". Her husband reinforced the ***blame*** for "not fighting the man off". When she slept with her husband, she had ***nightmares*** about the rape and woke up screaming. When they tried to have sex, it was difficult as Wanda kept ***'seeing'*** the man who had raped her. Wanda was unable to come to terms with the fact that she had become pregnant as a result of the rape and had an abortion which she saw as very wrong.

Initial counselling concentrated on Wanda's feelings of ***guilt*** and ***blame.*** These appeared to stem from her religious beliefs, which had taught her that it is very wrong to have sex with anyone other than the person she married, otherwise she would not be trustworthy. Wanda had also grown up with her mother and female teachers and had had little contact with men. She had accepted her husband because he went to church and so she felt he could be trusted. The lack of trust she now felt of herself was the centre of her feelings of guilt and she needed careful reassurance and long discussion before she was able to begin to see that she had not been responsible for encouraging the rape.

Wanda had recently seen an anti-abortion film on television and this had reinforced her feelings of guilt. As she was encouraged to talk about the abortion, it became apparent that her views on the subject were really quite liberal. When asked in what circumstances she would consider abortion to be permissible, she included cases of rape. In this way, she was in fact saying that her own termination had been for good reasons. She was able to agree with this and also felt that her husband could have accepted the rape in a better way if she had not become pregnant as a result.

Wanda became more able to rationalise her feelings about the termination as she realised that she would not have been able to keep the child because of her husband's feelings and because the baby would always have been a reminder of the rape.

When she was eventually able to accept that she was not responsible for the rape, Wanda was also able to discuss that it was the circum-stances in which it happened that worried her. She felt it would not have seemed so bad to other people if she had been attacked in a public place. She also felt that if this had been so, her husband would have found it easier to believe her side of the story.

Wanda found it difficult to express her feelings to people who were close to her. She seemed very frightened of men, and sex in general. Her very protected childhood and religious upbringing had encouraged her to repress her feelings. She tried always to be kind and not to hurt people, but this resulted in her being hurt herself. Wanda needed help in learning how to express her feelings appropriately and openly.

This case shows the need for patience, objectivity and understanding to encourage clients to open up in their own time and begin to realise the reasons for their ***anxiety, confusion*** and ***grief.***

Counsellors should be honest, unselfconscious and confident to draw out clients emotionally and allow them to confide in us. While doing this, we will need an ability to confront unpleasant reality and be prepared for clients blocking and being defensive. We may need to overcome a natural dread of hurting someone and to develop the ability to give honest feedback on different issues which clients might raise. It is sometimes easy to be too accepting and be overwhelmed by words - of course counsellors should be accepting and supportive listeners but they should also be able to provide structure for clients to grasp.

Counsellors require the ability to judge the ego-strength of clients so that they may assess the speed at which clients are progressing and when it is the right moment to move them on. Counsellors should be in control, without moving the client on unnecessarily. To do this, we may have to make the implicit explicit, and reinforce the reality of the situation.

Counsellors may need to exert considerable control and directness in order to keep clients talking about the problem in hand. Think now about separating the strands of the 'mess'. For example: "I'd like to get back to your major concern"; "How does this relate to the problems we are discussing?"; "I'm confused, I'd like to know more about...".

All the time, while we are looking toward catharsis (emotional cleansing) in clients and moving them on to a new equilibrium, we should be thinking about the dependency which the client may be building on the counsellor. The object of the exercise is to allow the client to become independent, for one day in the future we, the counsellors, will have to provide our clients with another loss - the withdrawal of the support we have given them, and of ourselves.

Closing

If our contract with our clients was properly negotiated, both they and we will have the understanding that the relationship will have to end sometime. There will be pressures on the counsellor's time to move on to other work with other clients. If the counselling process has been successful, then clients also may wish to move on to living their lives with their new-found normality, without the support of the counsellor.

It cannot be stressed strongly enough that the counsellor began work with a vulnerable client, suffering from loss, and susceptible to intervention. All through the counselling process, we should be watchful to prevent the client becoming too dependent on the counsellor; some clients will automatically become 'attached' to their counsellor through both an inability to support themselves and a gratitude for what the counsellor is doing for them. As soon as the client is making suitable progress towards a restoration of emotional equilibrium and functional ability, the counsellor should consider weaning the client off any dependency.

Face-to-face contact may be diminished over several months, although there may still be a need for less frequent monitoring of the client's progress, i.e. on birthdays, anniversaries and a year after the loss occurred. If, during counselling, we have noted the client's growth potential, and this is progressing reasonably and as expected, the counsellor may only need to 'top-up' the client's self-determination to progress with support at certain intervals.

Summary

To reaffirm what was stated in the introduction of this chapter, the stages of the counselling process do form a chronological progression. How far counsellors advance through this process will depend on our abilities to hold our clients and on the faith of our clients in what we are aiming to achieve for their sake.

What should be made clear is that counselling may not necessarily be unsuccessful if it started with the 'opening', but does not reach the 'closing' having passed through all the other stages. Both counsellor and client may agree not to proceed to the 'contract' stage or the 'working through grief' stage if they feel the client can manage without the counsellor's help. The initial stages of the process may work well enough, in their own right, to motivate the client to move forward alone.

Although some counsellors feel they should never give advice, this is too simple a view. Advice is appropriate on some occasions when counsellors are in a position to know they are right and on matters where the outcome is predictable. Clients might be advised about which agency they should contact for help with a particular difficulty. However, with more complex problems, giving advice which may not be taken up may complicate a relationship. Advice may well be ill-informed or improper if it leads clients to opt out of examining their own difficulties and the responsibility for their own actions.

Counsellors may often be surprised to discover that, after giving a full presentation of the advantages and disadvantages of a particular course of action, clients may say they have decided to follow the counsellor's advice, when none has really been given. However, such comments as "Since you think it best to..." may be a sign of the client's anxiety to avoid the responsibility of making personal decisions.

People in crisis are more dependent than usual, and therefore more susceptible to influence. This can present counsellors with opportunities and with risks. While relationships may be relatively easy to establish, counsellors need to guard against suggesting courses of action to a client who is not in a state to explore the implications, and who feels it is easier to do what the counsellor seems to think is best. Although a distressed client may need to have some limits set, the counsellor should not exploit the client's temporary dependence in order that they should do what the counsellor thinks is right.

Counsellors may be continually exposed to suffering; therefore it is essential that they recognise their own inadequacies. Be honest with yourself - when you say you want to protect the client from unpleasant reality, is it also true that you are protecting yourself from the client's upset reaction? We must learn to cope with our own anxiety for the benefit of the clients.

Counsellors who can acknowledge their own limitations no longer need to prove anything. They do not have to win any power games with their clients, have a need for their clients to like them or even try to impress their colleagues. They are able to be more effective because their own defences are minimised. They will have learned to be counsellors to themselves and this can relieve them of unnecessary stress and allow them to achieve a good involvement in their relationship with their clients.

Chapter Five

Summary & Postscript

In the Introduction of this book, I mentioned the experiences we all have in our lives which we can utilise to become counsellors. This basic experience, and an instinct to help others, will hopefully encourage people to learn more about the skills and techniques required for counselling and what may be expected of counsellors.

The concept for this book originated when I was producing a two-day course for in-service training for social workers. It seemed to me that, from a basic theory, counsellors need to rehearse and then perform the act of counselling. Therefore I tried to devise a programme that would, at least briefly, cover these three aspects.

In Chapter 1, a model of the Dimensions of Adjustment theory was presented which illustrates the process which mourning may take after a major loss. Once we are aware of what might be happening to a client who has suffered a loss, we are more able to pinpoint goals which they will need to reach in order to restore some sort of equilibrium. While still regarding the client as a whole person, it would seem easier to break down the components of personality so that the sections may be examined in depth. Here, I was trying to 'sort out the strands of a mess'.

I have stated that these Dimensions overlap considerably and there are several types of behaviour which may fit into more than one Dimension. This is not so important as the fact that we, as counsellors, will have noted that the behaviour exists in some part of the client's life. If we miss it in one Dimension, we could well pick it up in another. The Dimensions, as listed, are not sequential.

Once we have assessed the client's current situation, we may move on to look toward the client's future and the restoration of functional ability. Each Dimension has a goal towards which we, together with the client, need to aim. (See Table 1 on page 12)

It should not be forgotten that, although bereavement is the most obvious form of loss which all of us meet, the principles behind the Dimensions of Adjustment model may be adapted to any loss situation. This was highlighted in Chapter 2. If someone dies, it is not simply the body gone. If someone moves into an old people's home, it is not simply a change of address. If someone loses a hand in an accident, it is not only the loss of something with which we combed our hair. Any loss brings with it a range of different consequences to different people. Thus, to be useful as counsellors we need to seek out, from each individual client, how the specific loss is affecting that client uniquely.

Chapter 3 included exercises which can help open up communication between two people. They may be adapted to incorporate into our personal repertoire. To create new skills or adapt old skills requires practice. If counsellors are skilled at interviewing, they have the advantage of making a question and answer session seem like a continuous conversation.

Counselling should be a mutual event with give and take from both the client and the counsellor. A skilled counsellor should be taking the relevant information which is needed in order to assess the Dimensional Adjustment of the client, while giving the client the opportunity to relax and begin to come to terms with the loss.

Chapter 4 moved on to the implementation of the theory and the practice into a process for a plan of action for counselling. Although more sequential than the Dimensions, it may be used as a guide and adapted to the counsellor's way of working, personality and time available. Look upon it as a recipe which may have an ingredient that you are not keen on. You may leave that ingredient out completely, or substitute another which is more to your liking; only time and honest evaluation will tell you whether the result is just as palatable for the client.

If counsellors are to become more skilled, they may well need to modify their work as they progress in their careers, adding techniques here and dropping techniques there. The main ingredient for counsellors is to feel comfortable with their performance however it has been constructed.

One of the difficult things about counselling is that it is sometimes not easy to know whether it has done any good. The client who does not come back may be the one who has been helped and feels no need to come back. It could just as easily be that the client who does not come back is the one who feels little or no help is being gained during the sessions. Often the results are only evident in the new and more appropriate behaviour of the client.

As counsellors, we need to make time for regular and continued study. Because we may have attended various courses, this does not mean that we have completed our knowledge of the subject. All professionals can go on learning all through their careers and, no matter how much experience we have now, it is always helpful to be involved with new techniques and methods of intervention. Even if we are unable to attend regular courses, there is a great deal of information available in print.

What enables counsellors to communicate well with a client is their thorough knowledge of the underlying principles which guide their work. Counsellors who want to help the client sensitively and professionally continue to master theoretical frameworks.

Although it is important that counsellors identify themselves with each client's problem to the degree that they are seen to empathise rather than sympathise, it may not be difficult to reach a stage where the empathy is so strong that counsellors may begin to take the client's problem upon themselves. This is unlikely to be helpful, and counsellors should stand back sufficiently to be objective. However, standing too far back can create the impression of being remote, cool and lacking empathy. Each counsellor has to find the balance, the happy medium between these two extremes, and this comes best from training, practice and supervision.

Every counsellor needs a supervisor or senior colleague with whom cases can be discussed and strategies developed when required. A counsellor may need to examine how a particular interaction with a client has gone and may need time to reflect on the last session in order to be better prepared to assist the client at the next. A sign of a professional counsellor is his or her readiness to seek out continuing supervision, not only as support but also as a process of continuing education. This enables the counsellor to express his or her own true feelings and to explore motives. Supervision may also help the counsellor perceive the work with the client from a new vantage-point. Self-examination, which takes effort and time, is necessary for all counsellors who wish to continue effective work, for they must accept the limitations, human and professional, under which they operate.

There will be times when we meet clients whom we cannot help and who should be referred on to another agency. The counsellor must be able to recognise these situations and know when to say "No". Also, in order to ensure that there is adequate time for relaxation and recharging batteries, as well as for continuing personal development, counsellors will require to make what is often the most difficult decision, that of saying "No, I'm sorry".

Nevertheless, counselling work does have many rewards. Above all, it is a never-ending process for those counsellors who are able to adapt new theories, methods and techniques for the benefit of their clients and themselves.

Further Reading

Berne E; "Games People Play" (Penguin, 1967)

Biestek F P; "The Casework Relationship" (George Allen and Unwin, 1961)

Dominian J; "Marital Breakdown" (Pelican, 1968)

Hart N; "When Marriage Ends" (Tavistock Pubs, 1976)

Hinton J; "Dying" (Pelican, 1967)

Kubler-Ross E; "On Death and Dying" (Macmillan, 1969)

Laing R D; "Self and Others" (Pelican, 1971)

Parkes C M; "Bereavement - A Study of Grief in Adult Life" (Pelican, 1975)

Pincus L; "Death and the Family" (Pantheon, 1974)

Smith C R; "Social Work with the Dying and Bereaved" (Macmillan (BASW), 1982)

Wallerstein J S and Kelly J B; "Surviving the Breakup" (Grant McIntyre, 1980)